Imperium Press was founded in 2018 to supply students and laymen with works in the history of rightist thought. If these works are available at all in modern editions, they are rarely ever available in editions that place them where they belong: outside the liberal weltanschauung. Imperium Press' mission is to provide right thinkers with authoritative editions of the works that make up their own canon. These editions include introductions and commentary which place these canonical works squarely within the context of tradition, reaction, and counter-Enlightenment thought—the only context in which they can be properly understood.

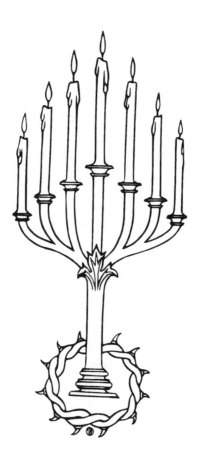

BALLADS WEIRD AND WONDERFUL

Edited by R. P. Chope
Illustrations by
Vernon Hill

PERTH
IMPERIUM PRESS
2021

Published by Imperium Press

www.imperiumpress.org

Ballads Weird and Wonderful published by
John Lane Co. 1912
in a limited edition of 500 copies

FIRST EDITION

A catalogue record for this
book is available from the
National Library of Australia

ISBN 978-1-922602-19-0 Paperback
ISBN 978-1-922602-20-6 EPUB
ISBN 978-1-922602-21-3 Kindle

Contents

Preface

THE scope of this book is sufficiently indicated by its title. The quality of the illustrations is not so patent, and for this reason I venture to claim attention from readers and critics in this introductory note.

Naturally, this is not a general collection of legendary ballads, and the slightly hackneyed themes of love and romance, so well known to us all, have not been touched upon in a volume intended only to deal with the weird and wonderful. Elves and fairies, demons and witches run riot through these pages and dance through the pictures. Here we have a revel of the bizarre, the whimsical, the extraordinary. Ballads of this type have a peculiar flavour of their own, which can be neither defined nor imitated, and they are, therefore, easily separable from the others. The subjects, moreover, are so strictly limited in number that it is thought the present collection contains typical specimens of all the best ballads of this character. They have not been taken from any single source, but many different versions have been consulted, and it is hoped that the resulting compilation gives the best obtainable.

Such a selection, it is believed, has not previously been published, but it was suggested as being peculiarly adapted to the genius of the artist of *The Arcadian Calendar* and *The New Inferno*. The result has more than justified the editor's expectations.

An artist who is not limited to the actual things of life, whose fancy is not confined within the limits of a green field or a marble column—who, indeed, can see visions—whose inner life is not of our life but of a strange occult devising, is impelled irresistibly towards the supernatural (though the word supernatural in connection with art should not be held only as indicating conditions above or below nature, but completely outside of and distinct from nature). Perhaps it is a lack of recognition of these several circumstances that causes us to condemn as morbid and decadent things which we are not in a position to judge. The word decadent is at once the most misused and the most overworked word in the English language. Any design that is not conventional, any picture that does not make an instant appeal by its prettiness—and that mere obvious prettiness the eye can take in completely at a glance—is liable to be misrepresented as decadent.

Mr. Hill's extraordinary art is neither conventional nor imitative. This is its great drawback. The desire to give every artist a professional pedigree confounds and irritates the mind that is accustomed to adjudicate in, and from, compartments: the mind that with a littleness of understanding is confused from its inability popularly to classify the subject criticised. In the same way there is a habit, proceeding from a mental obsession as much as from a spiritual blindness, to place every new poet as a legitimate or illegitimate descendant of Tennyson, Browning, or Wordsworth. And a new humourist is usually patted on the shoulder as a relative, though poor, of Thackeray, or Dickens, or Mark Twain. Mr. Hill is in this position: I have indicated rather than described it. There is in his work a suggestion of Blake, of Beardsley, and of Flaxman. There is something, perhaps, of Blake in the conception of Mr. Hill; there may be a touch of Flaxman in the execution; and possibly a trace of the exquisite delicate line of Beardsley in the symphonious whole. But what artist would deliberately choose to follow Blake, that most erratic genius? The Flaxman influence is even less significant. And Beardsley is dragged in more because Mr. Hill challenges Beardsley than that he follows him. But in any case it is no small compliment to an artist that he should be compared with three men of such talent. He is fortunately opposed to the gospel of the obvious—not in the flimsy manner of the post-impressionists, but with the lavish decoration of the master hand. These designs for *Ballads Weird and Wonderful* are indeed not only illustrations but decorations: they touch the soul with pity and with terror; they have the quality, the peculiar quality, of forming in the mind a permanent picture, long after the merely beautiful becomes an evanescent memory. Mr. Hill's work is such stuff as dreams are made of.

That Mr. Hill has been criticised for a certain morbid tendency is not altogether surprising. But it is impossible to produce designs for such a book without introducing a quality of grotesque, inverted melancholy. (This was most noticeable in Mr. Hill's very remarkable illustrations to *The New Inferno* of Mr. Stephen Phillips). I am strongly inclined to the belief that adverse criticism, on account of supposed morbidity, is usually produced by the modern habit of expressing a judgment of one thing in terms of another. Mendelssohn is condemned that his music does not noise like Wagner's; Mr. Abercrombie that his poetry has not Tennyson's smoothness; and it will never surprise me to see a book on political economy condemned as painfully deficient in humour! Even if one is unable to analyse the dexterities and attainments of certain people and several things, it is at least easy to evade the points at issue by demonstrating those qualities manifestly deficient, and that though such qualities would be incongruous in the persons or things criticised. And this artifice is without doubt superficially successful in concealing the intellectual poverty of the critic.

Certainly I shall be astounded if these wonderful drawings for *Ballads Weird and Wonderful* are not recognised as a triumph of modern art. Apart from their technique they reflect with marvellous fidelity the spirit of the ballads, the air of poetical mystery, the combination of the natural and the supernatural, the peculiar haunting beauty of the verses themselves.

R. P. CHOPE.

LONDON, *November* 28, 1911.

BALLADS WEIRD
AND WONDERFUL

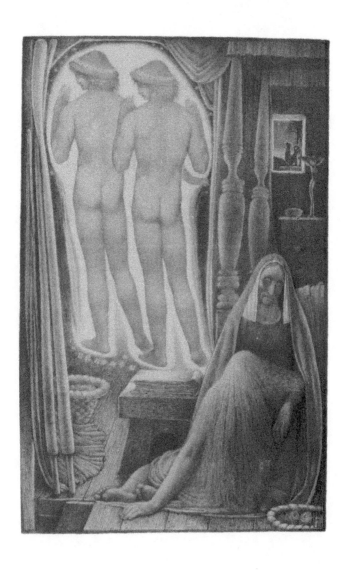

The Wife of Usher's Well

THERE liv'd a wife at Usher's Well,
    And a wealthy wife was she;
She had twa stout and stalwart sons,
    And she sent them o'er the sea.

They hadna been a week frae her,
    A week but barely ane,
When word came to the carline wife   *old peasant*
    That her twa sons were gane.   *woman*

They hadna been a week frae her,
    A week but barely three,
When word came to the carline wife
    That her sons she'd never see.

"I wish the wind may never cease,
    Nor freshes[1] in the flood,
Till my twa sons come hame to me
    In earthly flesh and blood!"

It fell about the Martinmas,[2]
    When the nights were lang and mirk,   *dark, gloomy*
When in and came her ain twa sons,

---

1 A flood, the overflowing of a river or stream.
2 St. Martin's Day, Nov. 11.

And their hats were o' the birk.   *birch*

It neither grew in syke[3] nor ditch,
    Nor yet in any sheugh;[4]
But at the gates of Paradise
    That birk grew fair eneugh.

"Blaw up the fire, now, maidens mine.
    Bring water frae the well.
For all my house shall feast this night.
    Since my twa sons are well.

"Oh, eat and drink, my merry men a',
    The better shall ye fare,
For my twa sons they are come hame
    To me for evermair."

And she has gane and made the bed,
    She's made it saft and fine;
And she's happit them in her grey mantle,   *covered*
    Because they were her ain.

Up then crew the red, red cock.
    And up and crew the gray;
And the aulder to the younger said,
    "Brother, we maun away.

"The cock doth craw, the day doth daw,   *dawn*
    The channerin' worm doth chide;   *fretful*
Gin we be missed out o' our place,
    A sair pain we maun bide."

Oh, it's they've ta'en up their mither's mantle.
    And they've hung it on a pin:

---

3   A small rill, especially one which runs dry in summer.
4   A small stream or open gutter running through land.

"Oh, lang may ye hing, my mither's mantle.   *hang*
    Ere ye hap us again!   *cover, enwrap*

"Fare ye weel, my mither dear!
    Fareweel to barn and byre!   *cow-house*
And fare ye weel, the bonny lass
    That kindles my mither's fire."

II

The Queen of Elfland's Nourice

"I HEARD a cow low, a bonnie cow low,
　And a cow low down in yon glen;
Lang, lang will my young son greet　　　　　*cry, lament*
　Or his mither bid him come ben.　　　　　*in, inside*

"I heard a cow low, a bonnie cow low,
　And a cow low down in yon fauld;　　　　*fold*
Lang, lang will my young son greet
　Or his mither take him frae cauld.

"Waken, Queen of Elfland,
　And hear your nourice moan."—　　　　　*nurse*

"O moan ye for your meat,
　Or moan ye for your fee,
Or moan ye for your bounties
　That ladies are wont to gie?"—

"I moan na for my meat,
　Nor yet for my fee,
But I moan for Christen land—
　It's there I fain would be."—

"O nurse my bairn, nourice,
　Till he stand at your knee,

An' ye'll win[1] hame to Christen land,
    Where fain it's ye would be.

"O keep my bairn, nourice,
    Till he gang by the hauld,[2]
An' ye'll win hame to your young son,
    Ye left when four nights auld."

1 *Win*, to succeed, especially in getting to a place.
2 *Gang by the hauld*, to walk by holding on to the hand.

III

The Demon Lover

"O WHERE hae ye been, my lang-lost love,
　　This lang seven years and more?"—
"O I'm come to seek my former vows
　　Ye granted me before."—

"O haud your tongue o' your former vows,
　　For they will breed sad strife;
Haud your tongue o' your former vows,
　　For I am become a wife."

He turn'd him right and round about,
　　And the tear blindit his ee;
"I ne'er wad bae trodden on Irish ground,
　　If it hadna been for thee.

"Had I kenn'd that ere I cam here,
　　I ne'er bad come to thee;
I might hae had a king's daughter,
　　Had it na been for love o' thee."—

"If ye might hae had a king's daughter,
　　Yoursell ye hae to blame;
Ye might hae taken the king's daughter,
　　For ye kenn'd that I was nane."—

"O fause are the vows o' womankind,
　　But fair is their fause bodie;
I ne'er wad hae trodden on Irish ground,

Had it na been for love o' thee."—

"If I was to leave my husband dear,
    And my twa babes also,
O what hae ye got to keep me wi',
    If I should wi' thee go?"—

"See ye not yon seven pretty ships,
    The eighth brought me to land,
With merchandise and mariners
    And wealth in ilka hand."

Then she's gane to her twa little babes,
    Kiss'd them baith cheek and chin;
Sae has she to her sleeping husband
    And done the same to him.

She set her foot upon the ship,
    No mariners could she behold;
But the sails were o' the taffetie,   *figured silk*
    And the masts o' beaten gold.

They hadna sail'd a league, a league,
    A league but barely three,
When dismal grew his countenance,
    And drumly grew his ee.   *dark, gloomy*

The masts that were like beaten gold,
    Bent not on the heaving seas;
The sails that were o' taffetie,
    Fill'd not in the east land breeze.

They hadna sail'd a league, a league,
    A league but barely three,
Until she espied his cloven hoof,
    And she wept right bitterlie.

"O haud your tongue, my sprightly flower,

Let a' your moanin' be;
I will show you how the lilies grow
   On the banks of Italy."—

"O what hills are yon, yon pleasant hills,
   That the sun shines sweetly on?"—
"O yon are the hills o' heaven," he said,
   "Where you will never win."—   *go*

"O whatten a mountain's yon," she said,
   "Sae dreary wi' frost and snow?"—
"O yon is the mountain o' hell," he cried,
   "Where you and I will go."

And aye when she turn'd her round about,
   Aye taller he seem'd to be;
Until that the tops o' that gallant ship
   Nae taller were than he.

The clouds grew dark, and the winds grew
  loud,
   And the tears fill'd her ee;
And waesome wail'd the snaw-white sprites   *dolefully*
   Upon the gurly sea.   *rough, stormy*

He strack the tapmast wi' his hand,
   The foremast wi' his knee;
And he brak that gallant ship in twain,
   And sank her in the sea.

IV

The Great Sealchie of Sule Skerrie

AN earthly nourice sits and sings,   *nurse*
    And aye she sings, "Ba, lily wean!   *little child*
Little ken I my bairn's father,
    Far less the land that he staps in."

Then ane arose at her bed-foot,
    And a grumly guest I'm sure was he: *grumbling*
"Here am I, thy bairn's father,
    Although I be not comèlie.

"I am a man upon the lan',
    And I am a sealchie in the sea;   *seal*
And when I'm far and far frae lan',
    My dwelling is in Sule Skerrie."[1]—

"It was na weel," quo' the maiden fair,   *quoth*
    "It was na weel, indeed," quoth she,
"That the Great Sealchie of Sule Skerrie
    Should hae come and aught a bairn to   *owned*
      me."

Now he has ta'en a purse of gowd,
    And he has put it upon her knee,
Saying, "Gie to me my little young son,

---

1 *Skerrie*, an isolated rock in the sea.

And tak' thee up thy nourice-fee.[2]

"And it shall pass on a summer's day,
 When the sun shines hot on every stane,
That I will take my little young son,
 And teach him for to swim the faem.   *foam, the sea*

"And thou shalt marry a proud gunner,
 And a proud gunner I'm sure he'll be,
And the very first shot that e'er he shoots,
 He'll shoot baith my young son and me."

2 The wages given to a wet nurse.

V

Alison Gross

ALISON GROSS, that lives in yon tower,
    The ugliest witch in the north countrie,
She trysted[1] me ae day up to her bower,
    And mony fair speeches she made to me.

She strok'd my head, and she kemb'd my
   hair,   *combed*
    And she set me down safely on her knee;
Says, "Gin ye will be my leman sae true,   *lover*
    Sae mony braw things I will you gie."   *smart,*
                                  handsome

She show'd me a mantle o' red scarlet,
    Wi' gowden flowers and fringes fine;
Says, "Gin ye will be my leman sae true,
    This goodly gift it shall be thine."—

"Awa', awa', ye ugly witch!
    Haud far awa', and let me be;   *hold*
I never will be your leman sae true,
    And I wish I were out o' your companie."

She neist brought a sark o' the saftest silk,
    Weel wrought wi' pearls about the band;
Says, "Gin ye will be my ain true-love,
    This goodly gift ye shall command."

1   *Tryst*, to engage to meet; to make an appointment to meet.

She show'd me a cup o' the good red gowd,
    Weel set wi' jewels sae fair to see;
Says, "Gin ye will be my ain true-love,
    This goodly gift I will you gie."

"Awa', awa', ye ugly witch!
    Haud far awa', and let me be;
For I wadna ance kiss your ugly mouth,
    For all the gifts that ye could gie."

She's turn'd her right and round about,
    And thrice she blew on a grass-green
      horn;
And she sware by the moon, and the stars
  aboon,   *above*
    That she'd gar me rue the day I was born.   *make*

Then out has she ta'en a silver wand,
    And she turn'd her three times round and
      round;
She mutter'd sic words, that my strength it
  fail'd,
    And I fell down senseless on the ground.

She turn'd me into an ugly worm,
    And gar'd me toddle[2] about the tree;   *wood*
And aye, on ilka Saturday night,
    Auld Alison Gross, she came to me,

With silver basin and silver kame,   *comb*
    To kemb my headie upon her knee;
But, ere I'd kiss'd her ugly mouth,
    I'd ha'e toddled for ever about the tree.

But it fell out last Hallowe'en,

---

2 *Toddle*, to walk with feeble, tottering steps.

When the seely court[3] was ridin' by,
The queen lighted down on a gowany[4] bank,
    Nae far frae the tree where I wont to lie.

She took me up in her milk-white hand,
    And she strok'd me three times o'er her
      knee;
She changed me again to my ain proper
  shape,
    And I nae mair toddle about the tree.

3 The fairy court, lit. the 'happy' court.
4 Covered with daisies.

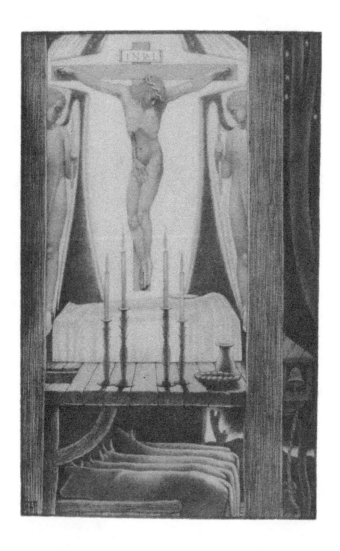

VI

A Lyke-Wake[1] Dirge

THIS ae nighte, this ae nighte,
　　Every nighte and alle,
Fire and sleet, and candle-lighte,
　　And Christe receive thy saule.　　　　　　　*soul*

When thou from hence away art past,
　　Every nighte and alle,
To Whinny-muir[2] thou com'st at last,
　　And Christe receive thy saule.

If ever thou gavest hosen and shoon,　　　　　*shoes*
　　Every nighte and alle,
Sit thee down, and put them on,
　　And Christe receive thy saule.

If hosen and shoon thou ne'er gav'st nane,
　　Every nighte and alle,
The whinnes sall prick thee to the bare bane,　*furzes : shall*
　　And Christe receive thy saule.

From Whinny-muir when thou may'st pass,
　　Every nighte and alle,
To Brig o' Dread thou com'st at last,　　　　　*bridge*
　　And Christe receive thy saule.

From Brig o' Dread when thou may'st pass,

1　The watch held over the dead between the time of death and burial.
2　A furze-covered moor.

Every nighte and alle,
To Purgatory fire thou com'st at last,
    And Christe receive thy saule.

If ever thou gavest meat or drink,
    Every nighte and alle,
The fire sail never make thee shrink,
    And Christe receive thy saule.

If meat or drink thou ne'er gav'st nane,
    Every nighte and alle,
The fire will burn thee to the bare bane,
    And Christe receive thy saule.

This ae nighte, this ae nighte,
    Every nighte and alle,
Fire and sleet, and candle-lighte,
    And Christe receive thy saule.

VII

The Twa Corbies

As I was walking all alane,
    I heard twa corbies making a mane;   *ravens : moan*
The tane unto the t'other say,   *that one*
    "Where sail we gang and dine to-day?"—

"In behint yon auld fail-dyke,[1]
    I wot there lies a new-slain knight;
And naebody kens that he lies there,
    But his hawk, his hound, and lady fair.

"His hound is to the hunting gane,
    His hawk to fetch the wild-fowl hame,
His lady's ta'en anither mate,
    So we may mak' our dinner sweet.

"Ye'll sit on his white hause-bane,   *collar-bone*
    And I'll pike out his bonny blue een;   *pick*
Wi' ae lock o' his gowden hair
    We'll theek our nest when it grows bare.   *thatch*

"Mony a one for him makes mane,
    But nane sall ken where he is gane;   *shall*
O'er his white banes, when they are bare,
    The wind sall blaw for evermair."

1   A wall or fence built of turf.

VIII

Kemp Owyne

HER mither died when she was young,
    Which gave her cause to make great
        moan;
Her father married the warst woman
    That ever liv'd in Christendom.

She servèd her wi' foot and hand,
    In everything that she could dee,   *do*
Till once, in an unlucky time,
    She threw her o'er a craig by the sea.

Saying, "Lie you there, dove Isabel,
    And all my sorrows lie with thee,
Till Kemp Owyne come to the craig,
    And borrow you wi' kisses three."

Her breath grew strang, her hair grew lang,
    And twisted round about a tree,
And all the people, far and near,
    Thought that a savage beast was she.

This news did come to Kemp Owyne,
    Where he did dwell, beyond the sea,
He hasted him to Estmere craig,
    And on the savage beast look'd he.

"O out o' my stithe I winna rise,   *place, station*
    And it is na for the fear o' thee,
Till Kemp Owyne, the kingis son,

Come to the craig and thrice kiss me."

Her breath was strang, her hair was lang,
   And twisted thrice about the tree,
And with a swing she came about:
   "Come to the craig, and kiss with me.

"Here is a royal belt," she cried,
   "That I have found in the green sea;
And while your body it is on,
   Drawn shall your blood never be;

"But if you touch me tail or fin,
   I swear my belt your death shall be."
He steppit in, gave her a kiss,
   The royal belt he brought him wi'.

Her breath was strang, her hair was lang,
   And twisted twice about the tree,
And with a swing she came about:
   "Come to the craig, and kiss with me.

"Here is a royal ring," she said,
   "That I have found in the green sea;
And while your finger it is on,
   Drawn shall your blood never be;

"But if you touch me, tail or fin,
   I swear my ring your death shall be."
He steppit in, gave her a kiss,
   The royal ring he brought him wi'.

Her breath was strang, her hair was lang,
   And twisted once about the tree;
And with a swing she came about:
   "Come to the craig, and kiss with me.

"Here is a royal brand," she said,   *sword*

"That I have found in the green sea;
And while your body it is on,
    Drawn shall your blood never be;

"But if you touch me, tail or fin,
    I swear my brand your death shall be."
He steppit in, gave her a kiss,
    That royal brand he brought him wi'.

Her breath was sweet, her hair grew short,
    And twisted nane about the tree,
And smilingly she came about,
    As fair a woman as fair could be.

IX

The Falcon

LULLY, lulley! lully, lulley!
    The faucon hath borne my make away!   *companion,*
    consort, 'mate'

He bare him up, he bare him down,
    He bare him into an orchard brown.

In that orchard there was an hall,
    That was hangèd with purple and pall.[1]

And in that hall there was a bed,
    It was hangèd with gold sae red.

And in that bed there li'th a knight,
    His woundès bleeding day and night.

At that bed's foot there li'th a hound,
    Licking the blood as it runs down.

By that bed-side kneeleth a may,   *maid*
    And she weepeth both night and day.

And at that bed's head standeth a stone,
    Corpus Christi written thereon.

Lully, lulley! lully, lulley!
    The faucon hath borne my make away.

1 A rich or fine cloth.

Sweet William's Ghost

LADY Marjorie, Lady Marjorie,
　　Sat sewing her silken seam;
By her came a pale, pale ghost,
　　With many a sigh and moan.

"Are ye my father, the King?" she says,
　　"Or are ye my brother John?
Or are you my true-love, Sweet William,
　　From England newly come?"—

"I'm not your father, the King," he says,
　　"No, no, nor your brother John;
But I am your true-love, Sweet William,
　　From England newly come."—

"Have ye brought me any scarlets sae red?
　　Or any silks sae fine?
Or have ye brought me any precious things,
　　That merchants have for sale?"—

"I have not brought you any scarlets sae red
　　No, no, nor the silks sae fine;
But I have brought you my winding-sheet,
　　O'er many a rock and hill.

"O Lady Marjorie, Lady Marjorie,
　　For faith and charitie,
Will you give to me my faith and troth,

That I gave once to thee?"—

"O your faith and troth I'll not give thee,
    No, no, that will not I,
Until I get ae kiss of your ruby lips,
    And in my arms you lie."—

"My lips they are sae bitter," he says,
    "My breath it is sae strang,
If you get ae kiss of my ruby lips,
    Your days will not be lang.

"The cocks are crowing, Marjorie," he says,
    "The cocks they are crowing again;
It's time the dead should part frae the quick,
    Marjorie, I must be gane."

She follow'd him high, she followed him low,
    Till she came to yon church-yard;
O there the grave did open up,
    And young William he lay down.

"What three things are these, Sweet
    William," she says,
    "That stand here at your head?"—
"It is three maidens, Marjorie," he says,
    "That I promis'd once to wed."—

"What three things are these, Sweet
    William," she says,
    "That stand here at your side?"—
"It is three babes, Marjorie," he says,
    "That these three maidens had."—

"What three things are these, Sweet
    William," she says,
    "That stand here at your feet?"—
"It is three hell-hounds, Marjorie," he says,

"That are waiting my soul to keep."

She's ta'en up her white, white hand,
    And she struck him in the breast,
Saying, "Have there again your faith and
    troth,
        And I wish your soul good rest."

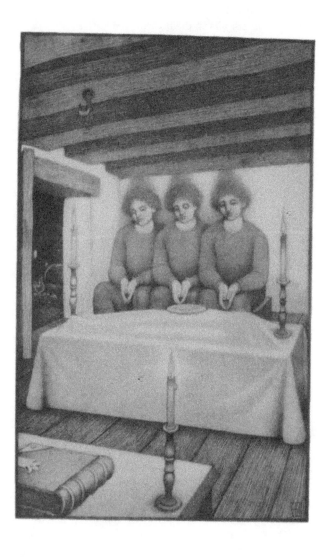

XI

Young Benjie

OF a' the maids o' fair Scotland,
    The fairest was Marjorie;
And young Benjie was her ae true-love,
    And a dear true-love was he.

And wow! but they were lovers dear,
    And lov'd full constantlie;
But aye the mair when they fell out,
    The sairer was their plea.   *quarrel*

And they hae quarrell'd on a day,
    Till Marjorie's heart grew wae;
And she said she'd choose another love,
    And let young Benjie gae.

And he was stout and proud-hearted,
    And thought o't bitterlie;
And he's gane by the wan moonlight
    To meet his Marjorie.

"O, open, open, my true-love;
    O, open, and let me in!"—
"I darena open, young Benjie,
    My three brothers are within."—

"Ye lee, ye lee, ye bonny burd,   *lie : young lady,*
    Sae loud's I hear ye lee;   *maiden*
As I came by the Lowden banks,

They bade gude e'en to me.

"But fare ye weel, my ae fause love,
   That I hae lov'd sae lang;
It sets ye choose another love,   *makes*
   And let young Benjie gang."

Then Marjorie turn'd her round about,
   The tear blinding her ee—
"I darena, darena let thee in,
   But I'll come down to thee."

Then saft she smil'd, and said to him—
   "O, what ill hae I done?"
He took her in his armès twa,
   And threw her o'er the linn.[1]

The stream was strang, the maid was stout,
   And laith, laith to be dang,   *loath : beaten*
But, ere she wan the Lowden banks,
   Her fair colour was wan.

Then up bespake her eldest brother—
   "O, see na ye what I do see?"
And out then spake her second brother—
   "It is our sister Marjorie."

Out then spake her eldest brother—
   "O, how shall we her ken?"
And out then spake her youngest brother—
   "There's a honey-mark[2] on her chin."

Then they've ta'en up the comely corpse,
   And laid it on the ground,

---

1   A waterfall, the rock or precipice over which the water falls.
2   A mole on the skin.

"O, wha has kill'd our ae sister.
    And how can he be found?

"The night it is her low lyke-wake,
    The morn her burial day,
And we maun watch at mirk midnight,   *dark, gloomy*
    And hear what she will say."

Wi' doors ajar, and candles light,
    And torches burning clear,
The streekit³ corpse, till still midnight,
    They wak'd, but naething hear.

About the middle o' the night
    The cocks began to craw;
And at the dead hour o' the night
    The corpse began to thraw.   *twist, contort,*
                                       'throw'

"O, wha has done thee wrang, sister,
    Or dar'd the deadly sin?
Wha was sae stout, and fear'd nae dout,
    As throw ye o'er the linn?"—

"Young Benjie was the first ae man
    I laid my love upon;
He was sae stout and proud-hearted,
    He threw me o'er the linn."—

"Shall we young Benjie head, sister?
    Shall we young Benjie hang?
Or shall we pike out his twa gray een,   *pick*
    And punish him ere he gang?"—

"Ye mauna Benjie head, brothers,
    Ye mauna Benjie hang,

---

3 *Streek*, to lay out a dead body.

But ye maun pike out his twa grey een,
    And punish him ere he gang.

"Tie a green gravat round his neck,   *cravat*
    And lead him out and in,
And the best ae servant about your house
    To wait young Benjie on.

"And aye, at every seven years' end,
    Ye'll take him to the linn;
For that's the penance he maun dree,   *endure, suffer*
    To scug his deadly sin."   *expiate*

XII

Edward, Edward

"WHY does your brand sae drap wi' blude,   *sword*
    Edward, Edward?
Why does your brand sae drap wi' blude?
    And why sae sad gang ye, O?"—
"O, I hae kill'd my hawk sae gude,
    Mither, mither:
O, I hae kill'd my hawk sae gude,
    And I hae nae mair but he, O."

"Your hawk's blude was never sae red,
    Edward, Edward:
Your hawk's blude was never sae red,
    My dear son, I tell thee, O."—
"O, I hae kill'd my red-roan steed,
    Mither, mither:
O, I hae kill'd my red-roan steed,
    That was sae fair and free, O."—

"Your steed was auld, and ye hae gat mair,
    Edward, Edward:
Your steed was auld, and ye hae gat mair,
    Some ither dule ye dree, O."—   *sorrow : endure,*
"O, I hae kill'd my father dear,   *suffer*
    Mither, mither:
O, I hae kill'd my father dear,
    Alas! and wae is me, O."—

"And whatten penance will ye dree for that,

Edward, Edward?
And whatten penance will ye dree for that?
 My dear son, now tell me, O."—
"I'll set my feet in yonder boat,
  Mither, mither:
I'll set my feet in yonder boat,
 And I'll fare o'er the sea, O."—

"And what will ye do wi' your towers and
 ha,
  Edward, Edward?
And what will ye do wi' your towers and ha',
 That were sae fair to see, O?"—
"I'll let them stand till they down fa',
  Mither, mither:
I'll let them stand till they down fa',
 For here never mair maun I be, O."—

"And what will ye leave to your bairns and
 wife,
  Edward, Edward?
And what will ye leave to your bairns and
 wife,
 When ye gang o'er the sea, O?"—
"The warld's room; let them beg through life,
  Mither, mither:
The warld's room; let them beg through life,
 For them never mair will I see, O."—

"And what will ye leave to your mither dear,
  Edward, Edward?
And what will ye leave to your mither dear?
 My dear son, now tell me, O."—
"The curse of hell frae me sall ye bear,   *shall*
  Mither, mither:

The curse of hell frae me sall ye bear,
  Sic counsels ye gied to me, O."

The Elfin Knight

THE Elfin Knight stands on yon hill,
    Blaw, blaw, blaw winds, blaw,
Blawing his horn baith loud and shrill,
    And the wind has blawn my plaid awa'.

"I wish that horn were in my kist,   *chest, coffin*
And the laddie here that I love best."

She had no sooner these words said,
When that the knight came to her bed.

"Thou art o'er young a maid," quoth he,
"Married wi' me thou ill would'st be."—

"I hae a sister younger than I,
And she was married yesterday."—

"Married wi' me if thou would'st be,
A courtesy thou must do to me.

"Ye maun make me a fine holland sark,
Without any stitching or needle-wark.

"And ye maun wash it in yonder well,
Where dew never wat, nor rain ever fell.

"And ye maun dry it upon a thorn
That never budded sin' Adam was born."—

"Now, sin' ye've ask'd some things o' me,

It's right I ask as many o' thee.

"My father left me an acre o' land,
Between the saut sea and the strand.   *salt*

"And ye maun plow 't wi' your blawing
    horn,
And ye maun saw 't wi' pepper corn.

"And ye maun harrow 't wi' a single tine,[1]
And ye maun shear 't wi' a sheep's shank
    bane.

"And ye maun barn 't in yon mouse-hole,
And ye maun thrash 't in your shoe-sole.

"And ye maun winnow 't in your loof,[2]
And ye maun sack it in your gluve.

"And ye maun dry 't without candle or coal,
And grind it fine without quern or mill.

"When ye've done, and finish'd your wark,
Come back to me, and ye'll get your sark!"

1 The tooth of a harrow.
2 The palm of the hand.

XIV

True Thomas

TRUE Thomas lay on Huntly bank,
    A ferlie he spied wi' his ee,   *wonder, marvel*
For there he saw a lady bright,
    Come riding down by the Eildon Tree.

Her skirt was o' the grass-green silk,
    Her mantle o' the velvet fine,
At ilka tett of her horse's mane   *lock*
    Hung fifty siller bells and nine.

True Thomas, he pu'd aff his cap,   *off*
    And louted low down to his knee: *bowed*
"All hail, thou mighty Queen of Heaven!
    For thy peer on earth I never did see."—

"O no, O no, Thomas," she said,
    "That name does not belong to me;
I am but the Queen of fair Elf-land,
    That am hither come to visit thee.

"Harp[1] and carp,[2] Thomas," she said,
    "Harp and carp along wi' me;
And if ye dare to kiss my lips,
    Sure of your body I will be."—

1 To play the harp.
2 To recite as a minstrel.

"Betide me weal, betide me woe,
    That weird shall never daunton me."   *fate : intimidate*
Syne he has kiss'd her rosy lips,
    All underneath the Eildon Tree.

"Now ye maun gae wi' me," she said,
    "True Thomas, ye maun gae wi' me;
And ye maun serve me seven years,
    Thro' weal or woe as may chance to be."

She mounted on her milk-white steed;
    She's ta'en True Thomas up behind;
And aye, whene'er her bridle rang,
    The steed flew swifter than the wind.

O they rade on, and farther on,
    (The steed gaed swifter than the wind)
Until they reach'd a desert wide,
    And living land was left behind.

"Light down, light down, now, True Thomas,
    And lean your head upon my knee;
Abide, and rest a little space,
    And I will show you ferlies three.

"O see ye not yon narrow road,
    So thick beset with thorn and brier?
That is the path of righteousness,
    Though after it but few enquire.

"And see ye not that braid, braid road,   *broad*
    That lies across the lilly leven?[3]   *lovely*
That is the path of wickedness,
    Though some call it the road to heaven.

---

3 A lawn, glade, open ground in a forest.

"And see ye not that bonny road,
    That winds about the ferny brae?   *bank, hillside*
That is the road to fair Elf-land,
    Where thou and I this night maun gae.

"But, Thomas, ye maun haud your tongue,
    Whatever ye may hear or see;
For, if ye speak word in Elfin-land
    Ye'll ne'er get back to your ain countrie."

And they rade on, and farther on,
    And they waded through rivers aboon the   *above*
      knee,
And they saw neither sun nor moon,
    But they heard the roaring of the sea.

It was mirk, mirk night, there was nae star-   *dark, gloomy*
  light,
    And they waded through red blude to the
      knee;
For a' the blude that's shed on earth,
    Rins through the springs o' that countrie.

Syne they came to a garden green,
    And she pu'd an apple frae a tree:
"Take this for thy wages. True Thomas;
    It will give thee the tongue that can never
      lee."—   *lie*

"My tongue is mine ain," True Thomas said,
    "A goodly gift ye wad gie to me!
I neither dought to buy nor sell,   *was able*
    At fair or tryst[4] where I may be.

"I dought neither speak to prince or peer,   *could*

4   A meeting-place, rendezvous.

Nor ask of grace from fair ladie."—
"Now haud thy peace!" the lady said,
    "For as I say, so must it be."

He has gotten a coat of the even cloth,[5]
    And a pair o' shoon of the velvet green; *shoes*
And till seven years were gane and past,
    True Thomas on earth was never seen.

---

5 Smooth cloth, evenly shorn.

XV

The Cruel Mother

SHE has ta'en her mantle her about,
   All alone and alonie O;
She has gane aff to the gude greenwood,   *off*
   Down by yon greenwood sidie O.

She has set her back unto an aik,   *oak*
First it bowed, and syne it brake.

She has set her back unto a brier,
Bonny were the twa babes she did bear.

She has ta'en out her little pen-knife,
And she's parted them and their sweet life.

She has howkit a hole, baith deep and wide,   *hollowed*
She has put them in baith side by side.

She has gane back to her father's ha',
She seem'd the lealest maid o' them a'.   *most upright*

As she lookit o'er the castle wa',   *wall*
She saw twa naked boys playing at the ba'.   *ball*

"O, bonny boys, gin ye were mine,
I would cleed ye in the satin fine.   *clothe*

"O, and I would cleed ye in the silk,
And wash you aye in morning milk."—

"O, cruel mither, when we were thine,

Ye did na prove to us sae kind,

"But out ye took your little pen-knife,
And parted us, and our sweet life.

"And now we're in the heavens sae hie,
　　All alone and alonie O;
And ye hae the pains o' hell to dree,　　　　　*endure, suffer*
　　Down by yon greenwood sidie O.

XVI

Tamlane

"O I forbid ye, maidens a',
    That wear gowd on your hair,
To come or gae by Carterhaugh,
    For young Tamlane is there."

But up then spake her, fair Janet,
    The fairest o' a' her kin:
I'll come and gang to Carterhaugh,
    And ask nae leave o' him."

She has kilted[1] her green kirtle[2]
    A little aboon her knee;   *above*
And she has braided her yellow hair
    A little aboon her bree.   *brow*

She's prink'd[3] hersell, and preen'd[4] hersell,
    By the ae light o' the moon,
And she's awa' to Carterhaugh,
    To speak wi' young Tamlane.

And when she came to Carterhaugh,
    She gaed beside the well,
And there she fand his steed standing,   *found*

1 *Kilt*, to tuck up the skirts.
2 A woman's outer petticoat or short skirt.
3 *Prink*, to dress smartly or gaudily.
4 *Preen*, to dress up, deck oneself out.

But he wasna there himsell.

She hadna pu'd a red, red rose,
    A rose but barely three,
When up and starts a wee, wee man,
    At Lady Janet's knee.

Says—"Why pu' ye the rose, Janet?
    What gars ye break the tree?   *makes*
Or why come ye to Carterhaugh
    Without the leave o' me?"—

"This Carterhaugh it is mine ain,
    My daddy gave it me;
I'll come and gang to Carterhaugh,
    And ask nae leave o' thee."

He's ta'en her by the milk-white hand,
    Amang the leaves sae green;
And sair and mickle was the love
    That fell the twa between.

He's ta'en her by the milk-white hand
    Amang the roses red;
And they hae vow'd a solemn vow
    Ilk ither for to wed.

"The truth ye'll tell to me, Tamlane,
    A word ye maunna lee: *lie*
Gin e'er ye was in holy chapel,
    Or sain'd[5] in Christentie?"—   *Christendom*

"The truth I'll tell to thee, Janet,
    A word I winna lee:

5 *Sain*, to make the sign of the cross; thus, 'to be sained,' to be baptized.

A knight me got, and a lady me bore,
    As well as they did thee.

"Randolph, Earl Murray, was my sire,
    Dunbar, Earl March, is thine;
We lov'd when we were children small,
    Which yet you well may mind.

"When I was a boy just turn'd of nine,
    My uncle sent for me,
To hunt, and hawk, and ride wi' him,
    And keep him companie.

"There came a wind out of the north,
    A sharp wind and a snell;   *cold, piercing, keen*
And a dead sleep came over me,
    And frae my horse I fell.

"The Queen of Fairies keppit me   *stopped*
    In yon green hill to dwell;
And I'm a fairy, lithe and limber—
    Fair lady, view me well.

"And I would never tire, Janet,
    In Elfin-land to dwell;
But aye, at every seven years,
    They pay the teind to hell;   *tithe*
And I'm sae fat and fair o' flesh,
    I fear 'twill be mysell.

"This night is Hallowe'en, Janet,
    The morn is Hallowday;[6]
And, gin ye dare your true-love win,   *gain*
    Ye hae nae time to stay.

6 All Saints' Day, Nov. 1.

"The night it is gude Hallowe'en,
    When fairy folk do ride,
And she that wad her true-love win,
    At Miles Cross she maun bide."—

"But how shall I thee ken, Tamlane?
    Or how shall I thee knaw,
Amang sae many unearthly knights,
    The like I never saw?"—

"The first company that passes by,
    Say na, and let them gae;
The neist company that passes by,
    Say na, and do right sae;
The third company that passes by,
    Then I'll be ane o' thae.

"First let pass the black, Janet,
    And syne let pass the brown;
But grip ye to the milk-white steed,
    And pu' the rider down.

"For I ride on the milk-white steed,
    Wi' a gowd star in my crown;
Because I was a christen'd knight,
    They gie me that renown.

"My right hand will be gloved, Janet,
    My left hand will be bare;
And thae's the tokens I gie thee—
    Nae doubt I will be there.

"They'll turn me in your arms, Janet,
    An ask and then an adder;   *newt, lizard*
But haud me fast, let me not pass,
    I'll be your bairnie's father.

"They'll shape me in your arms, Janet,

A toad and then an eel;
But haud me fast, nor let me gang,
   As you do love me weel.

"And next they'll shape me in your arms
   A dove, and then a swan;
And last they'll shape me in your arms
   A mother-naked man:
Cast your green mantle over me,
   I'll be mysell again."

Gloomy, gloomy was the night,
   And eerie was the way,
As fair Janet, in her green mantle,
   To Miles Cross she did gae.

About the dead hour o' the night,
   She heard the bridles ring;
And Janet was as glad o' that
   As any earthly thing.

And first gaed by the black, black steed,
   And then gaed by the brown;
But fast she gript the milk-white steed,
   And pu'd the rider down.

She pu'd him frae the milk-white steed,
   And loot the bridle fa';   *let*
And up there rase an elritch cry: *unearthly,*
   "He's won amang us a'!"   *frightful*

They shaped him in fair Janet's arms,
   An ask, and then an adder;
She held him fast in every shape
   To be her bairnie's father.

They shaped him in her arms at last
   A mother-naked man;

She cast her mantle over him,
 And sae her true-love wan.

Up then spak' the Queen o' Fairies,
 Out o' a bush o' broom:
"She that has borrow'd young Tamlane
 Has gotten a stately groom.

"But had I kenn'd, Tamlane," she says,
 "A lady wad borrow thee,
I wad hae ta'en out thy twa grey een,
 And put in twa een o' tree.

"Had I but kenn'd, Tamlane," she says,
 "Before ye cam' frae hame,
I wad hae ta'en out your heart o' flesh,
 And put in a heart o' stane.

"And had I but had the wit yestreen
 That I hae coft this day,   *bought*
I'd paid my teind seven times to hell
 Ere you had been won away!"

Lord Thomas and Fair Annet

LORD Thomas and fair Annet
    Sat all day on a hill;
When night was come, and sun was set,
    They had not talk'd their fill.

Lord Thomas said a word in jest,
    Fair Annet took it ill:
"I winna wed a tocherless lass   *without dowry*
    Against my ain friends' will."—

"If ye will never wed a wife,
    A wife will ne'er wed ye."—
Sae he is hame to tell his mither,
    And knelt upon his knee.

"O rede, O rede, mither," he says,
    "A gude rede gie to me;
O, shall I take the nut-brown bride,
    And let fair Annet be?"—

"The nut-brown bride has gowd and gear,
    Fair Annet she's gat nane;
And the little beauty fair Annet has,
    O, it will soon be gane."

And he has to his brother gane:
    "Now, brother, rede ye me;

O, shall I marry the nut-brown bride,
    And let fair Annet be?"—

"The nut-brown bride has owsen, brother,   *oxen*
    The nut-brown bride has kye;   *cows, kine*
I wad hae ye marry the nut-brown bride,
    And cast fair Annet by."—

"Her owsen may die i' the house, billy,   *brother*
    And her kye into the byre;   *cow-house*
And I shall hae nothing to mysell,
    But a fat fadge[1] by the fire."

And he has to his sister gane:
    "Now, sister, rede ye me;
O, shall I marry the nut-brown bride,
    And set fair Annet free?"—

"I'se rede ye take fair Annet, Thomas,
    And let the brown bride alane;
Lest ye should sigh and say, 'Alas!
    What is this I hae brought hame?'"—

"No, I will take my mither's counsel,
    And marry me out o' hand;
And I will take the nut-brown bride—
    Fair Annet may leave the land."

Up then rose fair Annet's father,
    Twa hours or it were day,
And he is gane into the bower,
    Wherein fair Annet lay.

"Rise up, rise up, fair Annet," he says,
    "Put on your silken sheen;   *shining*

---

1   A fat, clumsy woman.

Let us gae to St. Mary's kirk,   *church*
    And see that gay weddin'."—

"My maids, gae to my dressing-room,
    And dress to me my hair;
Where'er ye laid a plait before,
    See ye lay ten times mair.

"My maids, gae to my dressing-room,
    And dress to me my sark;
The ae half is o' the holland fine,
    The ither o' needle-wark."

The horse fair Annet rode upon,
    He amblit like the wind;
Wi' siller he was shod before,
    Wi' burning gowd behind.

Four-and-twenty siller bells
    Were a' tied to his mane;
Wi' ae tift[2] o' the norland wind   *north*
    They tinkled ane by ane.

Four-and-twenty gay gude knights
    Rode by fair Annet's side,
And four-and-twenty fair ladies,
    As if she had been a bride.

And when she came to Mary's kirk,
    She sat on Mary's stean: *stone*
The cleeding that fair Annet had on,   *clothing*
    It skinkled in their een.   *sparkled, shined*

And when she came into the kirk,
    She shimmer'd like the sun;   *shine*

2 A sudden breeze or gust of wind.

The belt that was about her waist,
    Was a' wi' pearls bedone.

She sat her by the nut-brown bride,
    And her een they were sae clear,
Lord Thomas he clean forgat the bride,
    When fair Annet she drew near.

He had a rose into his hand,
    And he gave it kisses three,
And reaching by the nut-brown bride,
    Laid it on fair Annet's knee.

Up then spake the nut-brown bride,
    And she spake wi' mickle spite:
"And where gat ye that rose-water,
    That does make ye sae white?"—

"O, I did get the rose-water
    Where ye will ne'er get nane,
For I did get that very rose-water
    Into my mither's wame.   *womb*

"Tak' back and wear your rose, Thomas,
    As lang as it will last;
For, like your love, its sweetness a'
    Will soon be gane and past."

When night was come, and day was gane,
    And a' were boun' to bed,
Lord Thomas and the nut-brown bride
    In chamber they were laid.

They were na weel lain down,
    And scarcely fa'n asleep,
When up and stands she, fair Annet,
    Just at Lord Thomas' feet.

"Weel brook ye o' your nut-brown bride,   *enjoy*
    Between ye and the wa';   *wall*
And sae will I o' my winding-sheet,
    That suits me best ava.   *of all*

"Weel brook ye o' your nut brown-bride,
    Between ye and the stock;
And sae will I o' my black, black kist,   *chest, coffin*
    That has neither key nor lock!

"Weel brook ye o' your nut-brown bride,
    And o' your bridal bed;
And sae will I o' the cauld, cauld mools,[3]
    That soon will hap my head."   *cover, enwrap*

Lord Thomas rase, put on his claes,   *clothes*
    Drew to him his hose and shoon;   *shoes*
And he is on to Annet's bower,
    By the lee light[4] o' the moon.

The firsten bower that he came to,
    There was right dowie wark;   *doleful*
Her mither and her three sisters
    Were makin' to Annet a sark.

The neisten bower that he came to,
    There was right dowie cheer;
Her father and her seven brethren
    Were makin' to Annet a bier.

The lasten bower that he came to,
    O, heavy was his care,
The dead candles were burning bright,

---

3   Mould, earth of a grave.
4   The word 'lee' has here an indefinite intensitive force, with the connotation of loneliness.

And fair Annet streekit there.   *laid out*

"It's I will kiss your bonny cheek,
    And I will kiss your chin;
And I will kiss your clay-cauld lip,
    But I'll ne'er kiss woman again.

"This day ye birl⁵ at Annet's wake,
    The white bread and the wine;
Before the morn at twal o'clock,   *twelve*
    They'll birl the same at mine."

The tane was buried in Mary's kirk,   *that one*
    The tither in Mary's quire,
And out o' the tane there grew a birk,   *that one : birch*
    And out o' the tither a brier.   *that other*

And aye they grew, and aye they drew,
    As they would fain be near,
And by this ye may ken right weel,
    They were twa lovers dear.

5 To pass bread and wine round the company.

The Croodlin' Doo

"O WHERE hae ye been a' the day,
　　My little wee croodlin' doo?"[1]—
"O I've been at my grandmother's;
　　Mak' my bed, mammy, noo."

"O what gat ye at your grandmother's,
　　My little wee croodlin' doo?"—
"I got a bonny wee fishie;
　　Mak' my bed, mammy, noo."

"O where did she catch the fishie,
　　My little wee croodlin' doo?"—
"She catch'd it in the gutter-hole;
　　Mak' my bed, mammy, noo."

"And what did she do wi' the fishie,
　　My little wee croodlin' doo?"—
"She boil'd it in a brass pan;
　　Mak' my bed, mammy, noo."

"And what did ye do wi' the banes o't,
　　My little wee croodlin' doo?"—
"I gied them to my little dog;

1　*Croodle*, to coo like a dove. *Croodlin' doo*, 'cooing dove,' a term of endearment.

    Mak' my bed, mammy, noo."

"And what did your little doggie do,
    My little wee croodlin' doo?"—
"He stretched out his head and feet, and   *died*
    dee'd;
    Mak' my bed, mammy, noo."

XIX

The Water o' Wearie's Well

THERE came a bird out of a bush,
    On water for to dine;
And, sighing sair, says the king's daughter,
    "O wae's this heart o' mine."

He's ta'en a harp into his hand,
    He's harpit them a' asleep;   *lulled*
Except it was the king's daughter,
    Wha ae wink couldna get.

He's loupin' on his berry-brown steed,   *leaping*
    Ta'en her on behind himsell;
Then baith rade down to that water
    That they call Wearie's Well.

"Wade in, wade in, my lady fair,
    Nae harm shall thee befall;
Aft times hae I water'd my steed
    Wi' the water o' Wearie's Well."

The first step that she steppit in,
    She steppit to the knee;
And, sighing says this lady fair,
    "This water's nae for me."—

"Wade in, wade in, my lady fair,
    Nae harm shall thee befall;

Aft times hae I water'd my steed
    Wi' the water o' Wearie's Well."

The neist step that she steppit in,
    She steppit to the middle;
"O," sighing says this lady fair,
    "I've wat my gowden girdle."—

"Wade in, wade in, my lady fair,
    Nae harm shall thee befall;
Aft times hae I water'd my steed
    Wi' the water o' Wearie's Well."

The neist step that she steppit in,
    She steppit to the chin;
"O," sighing says this lady fair,
    "That this should gar twa true-loves   *make*
      twin!"[1]—

"Seven kings' daughters I've drowned there,
    I' the water o' Wearie's Well;
And I'll make ye the eight o' them,
    And ring the common bell."—

"Since I am standing here," she says,
    "This dowie death to dee: *doleful : die*
One kiss o' your comely mouth,
    I'm sure wad comfort me."

He loutit him o'er his saddle bow,   *stooped, bent*
    To kiss her cheek an' chin;
She's ta'en him in her armès twa,
    And thrown him headlong in.

1 *Twin*, to separate one from the other; to part, sever.

"Sin' seven kings' daughters ye've drowned
  there,
    I' the water o' Wearie's Well,
I'll mak' ye the bridegroom to them a',
    And ring the bell mysell."

And aye she warsled, and aye she swam,   *struggle,*
    And she swam to dry land;   *'wrestle'*
And thankit God most cheerfullie,
    For the dangers she overcam.

The Wee, Wee Man

As I was walking all alane
 Between a water and a wa',   *wall*
There I spied a wee, wee man,
 And he was the least that e'er I saw.

His legs were scant a shathmont[1] lang, *scarcely*
 And thick and thimber was his thie,   *heavy*
Between his brows there was a span,
 And between his shoulders there was
  three.

He has ta'en up a mickle stane,
 And he flung 't as far as I could see;
Though I had been a Wallace wight   *fellow*
 I couldna liften't to my knee.

"O wee, wee man, but ye be strang!
 O tell me where your dwelling be?"—
"My dwelling's down by yon bonny bower;
 O will ye gae wi' me and see?"

On we lap, and awa' we rade,   *leapt*
 Till we came to a bonny green;
We lighted down to bait our steed,
 And out there came a lady sheen;   *dazzling*

---

1 Six inches: the measure of the fist with the extended thumb.

Wi' four-and-twenty at her back
    A' comely clad in glisterin' green;   *glittering*
Tho' the King of Scotland had been there,
    The warst o' them might hae been his
        queen.

On we lap, and awa' we rade,
    Till we came to a bonny ha';
The roof was o' the beaten gowd,
    And the floor was o' the crystal a'.

When we came to the stair-foot,
    Ladies were dancing jimp and sma';   *slender, elegant*
But in the twinkling of an ee,
    My wee, wee man was clean awa'.

Hugh of Lincoln

A' THE boys o' merry Lincoln
  Were playing at the ba';
And wi' them was the sweet Sir Hugh,
  And he play'd o'er them a'.

ball

He kick'd the ba' then wi' his foot,
  And keppit it wi' his knee,
Till even in at the Jew's window,
  He gar'd the bonny ba' flee.

*intercepted,
stopped
made*

Then out and cam the Jew's daughter:
  "Will ye come in and dine?"—
"I winna come in, and I canna come in,
  Without my play-feres nine.

*companion,
comrade*

"Cast out the ba' to me, fair maid,
  Cast out the ba' to me!"—
"Ye ne'er shall hae 't, my bonny Sir Hugh,
  Till ye come up to me."

She's gane unto her father's garden
  As fast as she could rin,
And pu'd an apple, red and green,
  To wile the young thing in.

She wil'd him into ae chamber,
  She wil'd him into twa;
She wil'd him into the third chamber,

And that was the warst ava.   *of all*

And she has ta'en out a little pen-knife,
    Hung low down by her gair;[1]
She has twin'd the young thing o' his life,   *parted*
    A word he ne'er spak' mair.

And out and cam the thick, thick blude,
    And out and cam the thin,
And out and cam the bonny heart's blude,
    There was nae life left in.

She laid him on a dressing-board,
    And dress'd him like a swine,
And laughing says: "Gae now and play
    Wi' your sweet play-feres nine!"

She row'd him in a cake o' lead;   *wrapped, rolled*
    Bade him—"Lie still there and sleep!"
She cast him in a deep draw-well,
    Was fifty fathom deep.

When bells were rung, and mass was sung,
    And a' the bairns cam hame,
When ilka lady had hame her son,
    The Lady Helen had nane.

She row'd her mantle her about,
    And sair, sair 'gan she weep,
And she ran into the Jew's castle,
    When they were a' asleep.

"My bonny Sir Hugh, my pretty Sir Hugh!
    I pray thee to me speak."—

1 A triangular strip of cloth, &c., inserted at the bottom of a garment.

"O lady, gae to the deep draw-well,
    Gin ye your son would seek."

Lady Helen ran to the deep draw-well,
    And knelt upon her knee:
"My bonny Sir Hugh, an ye be here,
    I pray thee speak to me!"—

"The lead it is wondrous heavy, mother,
    The well is wondrous deep;
A keen pen-knife sticks in my heart,
    A word I downa speak.

"But lift me out o' this deep draw-well,
    Put a bible at my feet,
And bury me in yon churchyard,
    And I'll lie still and sleep.

"Gae hame, gae hame, my mither dear,
    Fetch me my winding-sheet;
And at the back o' merry Lincoln,
    It's there we twa shall meet."

Now Lady Helen she's gane hame,
    Made him a winding-sheet;
And at the back o' merry Lincoln
    The dead corpse she did meet.

And a' the bells o' merry Lincoln
    Without men's hands were rung;
And ne'er was such a burial
    Sin' Adam's days begun.

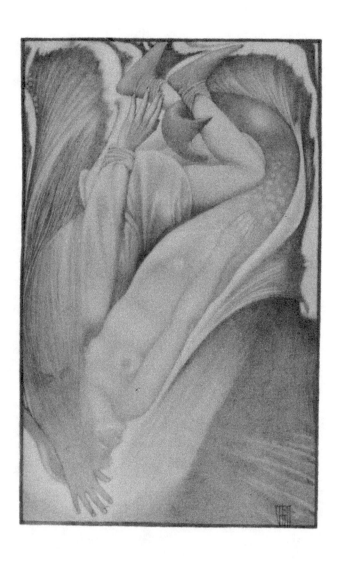

XXII

The Mermaid

To yon fause stream, that, near the sea,
    Hides many a shelf[1] and plum,[2]
And rives[3] wi' fearful din the stanes,
    A witless knight did come.

The day shines clear—far in he's gane
    Where shells are silver bright,
Fishes were loupin' a aroun',   *leaping*
    And sparklin' to the light.

Whan, as he laved, sounds cam sae sweet   *bathed*
    Frae ilka rock an' tree;
The brief was out,[4] 'twas him it doom'd
    The mermaid's face to see.

Frae 'neath a rock, soon, soon she rase,
    And stately on she swam,
Stopp'd i' the midst, and becked and sang
    To him to stretch his han'.

Gowden glist the yellow links   *gleamed*
    That round her neck she'd twine;
Her een war o' the skyie blue,

---

1 A reef or rock beneath the water.
2 A deep pool in a stream.
3 *Rive*, to split asunder, cleave.
4 *The brief was out*, the spell was cast.

Her lips did mock the wine;

The smile upon her bonny cheek
    Was sweeter than the bee;
Her voice excell'd the birdie's sang
    Upon the birchen tree.

Sae couthie, couthie did she look,   *kind, affable*
    And mickle had she fleech'd;   *coaxed, cajoled*
Out shot his hand—alas! alas!
    Fast in the swirl he screech'd.

The mermaid laugh'd, her brief was gane,   *spell, charm*
    And kelpie's[5] blast was blawin',
Fu' low she douk'd, ne'er rase again,   *ducked, dove*
    For deep, deep was the fawin'.   *falling*

Aboon the stream his wraith was seen,   *above : ghost*
    Warlocks tirl'd[6] lang at gloamin';   *wizards*
That e'en was coarse, the blast blew hoarse,
    Ere lang the waves were foamin'.

5 A water-spirit, "who gives previous intimation of the destruction of those who perish within his jurisdiction, by preternatural lights and noises, and even assists in drowning them".
6 *Tirl*, to make a rattling sound.

XXIII

Clerk Colvill

CLERK Colvill and his lusty dame
    Were walking in the garden green;
The belt around her middle jimp,   *slender, elegant*
    It cost Clerk Colvill pounds fifteen.

"O promise me now, Clerk Colvill,
    Or it will cost ye mickle strife,
Ride never by the wells of Slane,
    If ye wad live and brook your life."—   *possess, enjoy*

"Now speak nae mair, my lusty dame,
    Now speak nae mair of that to me;
For I ne'er did see a fair woman,
    That I did like sae weel as thee."

He's ta'en his leave o' his gay lady,
    Nought minding what his lady said,
And he's rode by the wells of Slane,
    Where washing was a bonny maid.

"Wash on, wash on, my bonny maid,
    That wash sae clean your sark o' silk;"—
"And weel fare you, fair gentleman,
    Your body whiter than the milk."

Then loud, loud cried the Clerk Colvill,
    "O my head it pains me sair;"—
"Then take, then take," the maiden said,

"And frae my sark you'll cut a gair."[1]

Then she's gied him a little bane-knife,
 And frae her sark he cut a share;
She's tied it round his whey-white face,
 But aye his head it achèd mair.

Then louder cried the Clerk Colvill:
 "O sairer, sairer aches my head;"—
"And sairer, sairer ever will,"
 The maiden laugh'd, "till you be dead."

Out then he drew his shining blade,
 Thinking to stick her where she stay'd,
But she was vanish'd to a fish,
 And swam far off, a fair mermaid.

He's mounted on his berry-brown steed,
 And dowie, dowie rade he hame,   *doleful*
And heavily, heavily lighted down,
 When to his lady's bower he came.

"O mither, mither, braid my hair;
 My lusty lady, make my bed;
O brother, take my sword and spear,
 For I hae seen the fause mermaid."

1 See footnote 1, p. 92.

XXIV

Sir Roland

WHEN he came to his ain love's bower,
    He tirlèd at the pin,[1]
And sae ready was his fair fause love
    To rise and let him in.

"O welcome, welcome, Sir Roland," she says,
    "Thrice welcome thou art to me;
For this night thou wilt feast in my secret
  bower,
    And to-morrow we'll wedded be."—

"This night is Hallowe'en," he said,
    "And to-morrow is Hallowday;[2]
And I dream'd a dreary dream yestreen,
    That has made my heart fu' wae.

"I dream'd a dreary dream yestreen,
    And I wish it may come to gude;
I dream'd that ye slew my best grewhound,   *greyhound*
    And gied me his lapper'd blude."   *clotted*

1 Doors were formerly provided with a long, notched iron handle on
which a loose iron ring was hung; instead of rousing the house with a
knock, the caller tirled the ring up and down the notches of the 'tirling
pin,' or handle, and produced the sound from which the apparatus
took its name.
2 All Saints' Day, Nov. 1

"Unbuckle your belt, Sir Roland," she said,
    "And set you safely down."—
"O your chamber is very dark, fair maid,
    And the night is wondrous lown."—   *quiet, calm,*
        silent

"Yes, dark, dark is my secret bower,
    And lown the midnight may be;
For there is none waking in a' this tower,
    But thou, my true-love, and me."

She has mounted on her true-love's steed,
    By the ae light of the moon;
She has whipped him and spurred him,
    And roundly she rade frae the toun.

She hadna ridden a mile frae the gate,
    A mile but barely ane,
When she was aware of a tall young man,
    Slow riding o'er the plain.

She turn'd her to the right about,
    Then to the left turn'd she,
And aye, 'tween her and the wan moonlight,
    That tall knight did she see.

And he was riding burd-alane[3]
    On a horse as black as jet;
But, though she follow'd him fast and fell,   *eagerly*
    No nearer could she get.

"O stop! O stop! young man," she said,
    "For I in dule am dight;   *sorrow: dressed*
O stop, and win a fair lady's love,
    If ye be a leal true knight."   *upright, honest*

3 Entirely alone, all alone.

But nothing did the tall knight say,
    And nothing did he blin;   *stop*
Still slowly rade he on before,
    And fast she rade behind.

She whipp'd her steed, she spurr'd her steed,
    Till his breast was all a-foam;
But nearer to that tall young knight,
    By Our Lady, she could not come.

"O if ye be a gay young knight,
    As well I trow you be,   *trust*
Pull tight your bridle reins, and stay
    Till I come up to thee."

But nothing did that tall knight say,
    And no whit did he blin,   *stop*
Until he reach'd a broad river's side,
    And there he drew his rein.

"O is this water deep?" he said,
    "As it is wondrous dun;[4]
Or is it sic as a sackless maid   *innocent*
    And a leal true knight may swim?"—

"The water it is deep," she said,
    "As it is wondrous dun;
But it is sic as a sackless maid
    And a leal true knight may swim."

The knight spurr'd on his tall black steed;
    The lady spurr'd on her brown;
And fast they rade into the fleed,   *flood, river*
    And fast they baith swam down.

4 A yellowish-brown colour.

"The water weets my tae," she said;   *wets*
    "The water weets my knee;
Haud up my bridle reins, sir knight,   *hold*
    For the sake of Our Ladie."—

"If I should help thee now," he said,
    "It were a deadly sin,
For I have sworn ne'er to trust a fair may's   *maid's*
    word,
    Till the water weets her chin."—

"O the water weets my waist," she said,
    "Sae does it weet my skin;
And my aching head rins round about,
    The burn makes sic a din.

"The water is waxing deeper still,
    Sae does it wax mair wide;
And aye the farther we ride on,
    Farther off is the other side.

"O help me now, thou fause, fause knight,
    Hae pity on my youth,
For now the water jows o'er my head,   *surges*
    And it gurgles in my mouth."

The knight turn'd right and round about,
    All in the middle stream;
And he stretch'd out his hand to that lady,
    But loudly she did scream.

"O this is Hallow-morn," he said,
    "And it is your bridal day;
But sad would be that gay wedding,
    If the bridegroom were away.

"Then ride on, ride on, proud Margaret,
    Till the water comes o'er your bree;   *brow*

For the bride maun ride deep, and deeper yet,
    That rides this ford wi' me.

"Turn round, turn round, proud Margaret,
    Turn round, and look on me;
Thou hast kill'd a true knight under trust,
    And his ghost now links wi' thee."

XXV

Willy's Lady

WILLY has ta'en him o'er the faem,   *foam, the sea*
He's woo'd a wife, and brought her hame;
He's woo'd her for her yellow hair,
But his mither wrought her mickle care;

And mickle dolour gar'd her dree,   *made : endure,*
For lighter she can never be;   *suffer*
But in her bower she sits wi' pain,
And Willy mourns o'er her in vain.

Arid to his mither he has gane,
That vile rank witch of vilest kind.

He says, "My lady has a cup,
Wi' gowd and silver set about;
This goodly gift shall be your ain,
And let her be lighter of her bairn."—

"Of her bairn she'll never be lighter,
Nor in her bower to shine the brighter;
But she shall die, and turn to clay,
And you shall wed another may."—   *maid*

"Another may I'll ne'er wed nane,
Another may I'll ne'er bring hame;"
But, sighing, says that weary wight,   *creature,*
"I wish my life were at an end!"—   *person, fellow*

"Yet gae ye to your mither again,

That vile rank witch of vilest kind,
And say your lady has a steed,
The like of him's no in the lands of Leed.

"For at ilka tett o' that horse's mane,   *lock*
There's a gowden chess,[1] and a bell to ring;
This goodly gift shall be her ain,
And let me be lighter of my bairn."—

"Of her bairn she'll never be lighter,
Nor in her bower to shine the brighter;
But she shall die, and turn to clay,
And you shall wed another may."—

"Another may I'll ne'er wed nane,
Another may I'll ne'er bring hame;"
But, sighing, says that weary wight,
'I wish my life were at an end!"—

"Yet gae ye to your mither again,
That vile rank witch of vilest kind,
And say your lady has a girdle,
It's a' red gowd unto the middle,

"And aye, at ilka siller hem,
Hang fifty siller bells and ten;
This goodly gift shall be her ain,
And let me be lighter of my bairn."—

"Of her bairn she'll never be lighter,
Nor in her bower to shine the brighter;
But she shall die, and turn to clay,
And you shall wed another may."—

"Another may I'll ne'er wed nane,

1 Leather strap for a hawk's leg.

Another may I'll ne'er bring hame;"
But, sighing, says that weary wight,
"I wish my life were at an end!"

Then out and spake the billy-blin,[2]
And he spake out in very good time:

"Yet gae ye to the market-place,
And there buy ye a loaf of wace;   *wax*
Ye'll shape it bairn and bairnly like,
And in't twa glassen een ye'll put;

"And bid her your boy's christ'nin' to,
Then notice weel what she shall do;
And do you stand a little away,
And notice weel what she will say,"

He did him to the market-place,
And there he bought a loaf of wace;
He shaped it bairn and bairnly like,
And in't twa glassen een he put.

He did him to his mither then,
And bade her to his boy's christ'nin';
And he did stand a little away,
And noticed weel what she did say.

"O wha has loos'd the nine witch-knots,[3]
That were amang that lady's locks?
And wha's ta'en out the kames o' care,   *combs :*
That were amang that lady's hair?   *mountain ash*

"And wha has ta'en down that bush o'
    woodbine,

2   A household sprite or brownie, who performs kind services at night.
3   A matted lock of hair, supposed to be produced by witchcraft.

That hung between her bower and mine?
And wha has kill'd the master kid,
That ran beneath that lady's bed?
And wha has loos'd her left foot shee,   *shoe*
And let that lady lighter be?"

Syne Willy's loos'd the nine witch-knots,
That were amang that lady's locks;
And Willy's ta'en out the kames o' care,
That were amang that lady's hair;

And he's ta'en down the bush o' woodbine,
Hung atween her bower and the witch   *old peasant*
 carline;   *woman*
And he has killed the master kid,
That ran beneath that lady's bed;

And he has loos'd her left foot shee,
And let that lady lighter be;
And now he has gotten a bonny son,
And mickle grace be him upon.

Glossary of Common Terms

Ae, one, only
Ain, own
An, if
Ane, one
Awa', away

Baith, both
Bane, bone
Bower, chamber

Ee, eye; *een*, eyes

Fause, false
Frae, from

Gae, gang, to go.
Gie, give
Gin, if
Gowd, gold
Gude, good

Hae, have
Haud, hold
Hie, high

Ilka, each, every

Ken, to know

Mair, more
Maun, must
Mickle, much, great

Neist, next

Pu', pull

Rade, rode, pret. of 'ride'
Rase, rose, pret. of 'rise'
Rede, to advise; advice

Sair, sore
Sark, shirt
Sic, such
Siller, silver
Sin', since
Stout, haughty
Syne, afterwards, next in point of time

Thie, thigh
Twa, two

Wad, would
Wae, woe
Winna, will not

Yestreen, last night, 'yester-even'

CPSIA information can be obtained
at www.ICGtesting.com
Printed in the USA
LVHW091205051121
702532LV00010B/829